The universe created you
for a reason; now go out there
and find out what it is.

NIKITA GILL

The things we lose are not losses.
They are entryways.

BRIANNA WIEST

When the world is quiet
and you're truly alone
and with your mind,
what do you think about?
What do you hope for?
Follow that.

BIANCA SPARACINO

What if you just accepted,
for this moment,
that you do not have to be perfect?

CHRISSY STOCKTON

Give yourself credit.

You are doing so much better than you think you are. You are so much more accomplished than you know.

BRIANNA WIEST

You are not broken.
You're becoming.

BIANCA SPARACINO

Be easy on your soul;
it needs softness,
it needs time,
it needs patience.

NIKITA GILL

When nothing is known, anything is possible.

JEREMY GOLDBERG

You're allowed to leave any story
you don't find yourself in.

You're allowed to leave any story
you don't love yourself in.

RANIA NAIM

In life, always strive to be
the kind of person who can see
humans at their worst and still
love them, because that is when
they need love the most.

NIKITA GILL

There's nothing wrong with being vulnerable. Vulnerability is a sign of strength, not weakness.

RANIA NAIM

Maybe you were the hero
you were waiting for; maybe you
were the love of your life all along.

BRIANNA WIEST

Let it hurt.
Let it bleed.
Let it heal.
And let it go.

NIKITA GILL

All of the love you have given to the wrong people—it will find its way back to you.

BIANCA SPARACINO

You are braver than you think, and sharing weakness is a sign of strength.

Weakness that is acknowledged, accepted, and shared is not weakness at all. It is courage. It is brave. It is strength.

JEREMY GOLDBERG

Relax. You will become an adult. You will figure out your career. You will find someone who loves you. You have a whole lifetime; time takes time. The only way to fail at life is to abstain.

CHRISSY STOCKTON

Love someone who is
kinder to you
than you are to yourself.

NIKITA GILL

Express, express, express.

Open yourself up, do not harden yourself to the world, and be bold in who, and how, you love.

There is courage in that.

BIANCA SPARACINO

THOUGHT
CATALOG
Books